TEAMS-GAMES-TOURNAMENT: THE TEAM LEARNING APPROACH

The Instructional Design Library
Volume 37

TEAMS-GAMES-TOURNAMENT:
THE TEAM LEARNING APPROACH

David L. DeVries
Robert E. Slavin
Gail M. Fennessey
Keith J. Edwards
Michael M. Lombardo

Danny G. Langdon
Series Editor

**Educational Technology Publications
Englewood Cliffs, New Jersey 07632**

Library of Congress Cataloging in Publication Data

Main entry under title:

Teams-games-tournament.

 (The Instructional design library; v. 37)
 Bibliography: p.
 1. Educational games. 2. Team learning approach in education. I. DeVries, David L. II. Series: Instructional design library; v. 37.
LB1029.G3T4 371.3 79-26378
ISBN 0-87778-157-5

Copyright © 1980 Educational Technology Publications, Inc., Englewood Cliffs, New Jersey 07632.

All rights reserved. No part of this book may be reproduced or transmitted, in any form or by any means, electronic or mechanical, including photocopying, recording, or by any information storage and retrieval system, without permission in writing from the Publisher.

Copyright is claimed until March 1, 1990. Thereafter all portions of this work covered by this copyright will be in the public domain.

This work was developed under a contract with (or grant from) the National Institute of Education, Department of Health, Education, and Welfare. However, the content does not necessarily reflect the position or policy of the Agency, and no official endorsement of these materials should be inferred.

Printed in the United States of America.

Library of Congress Catalog Card Number: 79-26378.

International Standard Book Number: 0-87778-157-5.

First Printing: March, 1980.

FOREWORD

One day my daughter came home from school rather excited about a particular activity in her math class. She was looking with anticipation to the reoccurrence of this activity in her classroom. I surmised that she had not only learned some subject matter, but also had been motivated and was happy. She had just experienced and was looking forward to an instructional game which had been played on a team basis. Such excitement is rare, even though I am confident that her school is an excellent one. If TGT has some of these results, and I believe it does, and more, then truly it is an instructional design worthy of serious consideration.

As the authors make abundantly clear, one of the problems associated with instructional designs that purport to enhance group activity is that what is designed as a group activity generally ends up being the activity of just a few—usually the activity of those students who need it less than those who don't participate. TGT enhances the participation of all group members. It promotes participation, and it does so in the context of what the authors so well label the "cooperative reward structure."

I should like to commend the authors for a well-presented explanation of this instructional design. The reader will find the guide to the design components and implementation procedure to be clear, concise, and highly useful in his or her own development and implementation efforts.

Danny G. Langdon
Series Editor

PREFACE

In a recent "Peanuts" cartoon, Peppermint Patty asks her teacher a question which, as she says "... has bothered every kid who has ever gone to school. Why do you *never* call on me when I know the answer, but *always* when I don't?" What Peppermint Patty finds vexing about her classroom is not the particular curriculum or academic material which she is required to learn, but the way her level of knowledge is tested. She is dealing with issues of classroom task and reward structures. In particular, Peppermint Patty is complaining that the reward structure of the classroom is insensitive to her efforts—she fails to be rewarded when she knows the answer. We should not be surprised when she stops doing the work required to know the answers. This book explains an alternative classroom structure—Teams-Games-Tournament—which can provide the Peppermint Patties of the nation's classrooms with a more motivating and satisfying experience.

CONTENTS

FOREWORD v

PREFACE vii

ABSTRACT xi

    I.   USE 3

   II.   OPERATIONAL DESCRIPTION 9

  III.   DESIGN FORMAT 21

  IV.   OUTCOMES 59

   V.   DEVELOPMENTAL GUIDE 67

  VI.   RESOURCES 73

 VII.   APPENDIX A: Sample Items 77

VIII.   APPENDIX B: Sample Newsletter 87

ABSTRACT

TEAMS-GAMES-TOURNAMENT

Teams-Games-Tournament (TGT) is a structure for reorganizing the classroom into four- or five-member teams, each having members from all levels of achievement. A rank-ordering procedure is used to form teams of comparable ability. The teams sit together and regularly engage in peer tutoring sessions in preparation for TGT tournaments. Skill exercise games are played during weekly tournaments. They focus on the objectives being taught at the time. During the games, students compete individually as representatives of their teams against two or three other students of comparable ability. At each game table, the contesting students answer questions to demonstrate mastery of specific skills. Points are awarded on the basis of performance at each table so that low-achieving students can score just as many or more points for their teams as high-achieving students.

Research on TGT in classroom experiments shows a clear pattern of increase in academic achievement, student satisfaction with the class, peer tutoring/mutual concern among students, cross-racial cooperation, and subject-matter understanding.

This narrative includes the theory and research on TGT and a detailed explanation of its implementation in the classroom.

TEAMS-GAMES-TOURNAMENT: THE TEAM LEARNING APPROACH

I.
USE

What Is TGT?

Teams-Games-Tournament is a carefully structured sequence of teaching-learning activities, a blend of three educational techniques—small groups, instructional games, and tournaments. It is designed to complement regular instruction in upper elementary, junior, and senior high school classrooms. The purpose of TGT is to create an effective classroom environment in which all students are actively involved in the teaching-learning process and consistently receive encouragement for successful performance. The TGT structure embodies both competition and cooperation in a way that promotes peer group rewards for academic achievement. It does this by altering the social organization of the classroom in two ways. First, it creates an interdependency among students. Second, it makes it possible for all students, despite different learning rates, to have an equal chance to succeed at an academic task.

To help you understand how TGT works in the classroom, each of its three basic elements will be described briefly.

Teams. Students are assigned to four-member teams. Within each team, there are students from all achievement levels. Ideally, each team has one high-achieving student, two average-achieving students, and one low-achieving student. However, the average achievement of each team should be approximately equal. During the time when TGT is used, preferably a semester, the membership of the teams remains intact. Each team has one or two practice sessions each week during which teammates tutor each other on classroom work.

Games. Skill-exercise games are played during weekly tournaments. They focus on the objectives being taught at the time.

Tournament. Over a period of time, the students play the game at least once a week. Teams do not compete as teams; rather, each team member is assigned to a tournament table to compete against two other students, each representing a different team. At any tournament table, the three students are roughly comparable in achievement level. The tournament tables are numbered and arranged in a hierarchy, with Table No. 1 being the top table. At the end of the period, the players at each table compare their scores to determine the top scorer, middle scorer, and low scorer. The game scores are converted into points, with a fixed number of points assigned to the top scorers, middle scorers, and low scorers at the various tables; there is also a provision for assigning points in case of a tie.

The points that the players earn are used in two ways. First, they determine who will be "bumped" up to the next highest table in the hierarchy, who will be "bumped" down to the next lowest table, and who will remain at the same table the next time the tournament is played. Second, a player's points are added to those that the other members of the player's team earn to compute a team score. The individual and team scores are ranked and listed in a tournament newsletter, copies of which are distributed to the class the day following the tournament.

What Is TGT Used For?

TGT has a flexible design which can be used for individualized learning, independent learning, and group instruction. Its focus is on individual performance, which in turn contributes to group performance.

As a teaching method, TGT "works" for several reasons. First, it capitalizes on the cooperative aspects of small groups, the motivational nature of instructional games, the competitive spirit of tournaments, and the students' familiarity with all of these. Second, TGT is inexpensive. It does not require costly materials or special facilities. TGT uses only materials and equipment available in most schools—even those whose budgets are limited—and it is at home in any kind of physical classroom structure. Third, TGT is easy to implement. It is designed to be used in 30- to 45-minute class periods, in any subject, with elementary and secondary school students, in conventional and experimental classroom arrangements. And, it can be used with equal success by both novice and veteran teachers.

TGT is a classroom technique that can help to make important and widespread changes in students' attitudes and achievement. Specifically, research on TGT in ten classroom experiments to date has demonstrated its usefulness to:

• *Increase academic achievement.* Learning basic facts and skills, such as mathematics tables and English grammar, has always implied an element of drudgery. The TGT structure relieves the drudgery of memorization and drill by making these part of the game-playing process. Students are more willing to work at the task and to increase their achievement levels.

• *Improve student attitudes.* TGT creates a sense of urgency and purpose in the students, both in the classroom and when they are outside it. For example, students become concerned about their attendance and classwork. This sense of purpose typically produces a more favorable attitude toward classmates and the subject matter at hand. In short, TGT gets students highly involved in the classwork and lets them enjoy the work.

- *Create student peer tutoring.* Through use of team grades, TGT fosters active tutoring among students. Particularly within their teams, students show an active and positive concern for each other's academic progress in the class. It becomes important to the students that their teammates consistently be present in class and that they be well-prepared. Given the opportunity, teammates translate this mutual concern into actual tutoring. The students themselves have shown an uncanny ability to assess who on the team needs the most help, on what skills assistance is needed, and who is the best individual to do the tutoring.

- *Simulate the outside world.* The TGT reward structure, which involves intense cooperation within a team and competition across teams, creates a classroom organization that closely resembles the organization of the world outside the classroom. Observers of recent changes note that our society is no longer based on competition among individuals, but depends heavily upon successful competition at the group level (see, for example, John Kenneth Galbraith, *The New Industrial State*). Because TGT requires students to cooperate with others on small work-oriented teams, shifting competition to the group level, it is a closer approximation of the society that students will face in the future. To that degree, TGT prepares students to operate in other organizational contexts.

- *Dissolve social barriers.* TGT can reduce the natural social barriers present in classrooms which include students from a variety of backgrounds. For example, using biracial teams represents perhaps the best way of truly integrating a desegregated classroom. Students of different backgrounds, placed together on a team, will work together for a common goal. Through such activities, social or other differences are blurred, and common interests and skills become more apparent.

Why TGT Works

1. TGT changes the way students work on academic tasks. Learning becomes social as children tutor one another and demonstrate their knowledge in public.

2. TGT also increases the types of rewards students receive. They get individual recognition and support for being a member of a team. Children learn how to work together in getting a job done and experience the good feelings which can come with sharing relationships.

3. In TGT, students compete only against their equals. Every student can succeed if he or she masters the subject matter contained in the games. This differs from the usual classroom arrangement, where learning is solitary and students are rewarded for doing better than everyone else whether they are at the same ability level or not.

4. TGT works because it motivates children to learn, even overlearn. It increases both their chance of success and the importance they attach to success. Children with differing abilities and skills cooperate and equals compete—the same things we're asked to do in life.

In the adult world, janitors don't compete with corporation presidents, and duffers don't compete with Jack Nicklaus. Such situations are inconceivable for adults, but we ask children to perform in this manner every day.

II.

OPERATIONAL DESCRIPTION

A classroom may be seen as being composed of two essential elements: a *task structure* and a *reward structure*. The task structure of a classroom refers to the instructional activities formed by the teacher. In most elementary and secondary classrooms, a variety of task structures may be used by the same teacher. Most school tasks involve students working alone (for example, completing worksheets or reading silently) or listening to or interacting with the teacher. A much smaller number of tasks involves students working or interacting with each other.

The reward structure of the classroom refers to the means that teachers use to motivate students to perform school tasks. Some tasks are intrinsically interesting to students, but even in the most free of free schools the teacher must recognize and reward appropriate student behavior if such behavior is to occur. In most classrooms, the major rewards used are teacher praise and grades. Teachers typically administer these rewards using multiple criteria. Most grades are based on (1) the comparison of a student's performance to that of his or her classmates; (2) a comparison of that student's performance with the teacher's idea of what the student should have accomplished (effort); and (3) such factors as attitude, neatness, classroom behavior, and the like. Informal teacher praise is administered according to the same general criteria.

One important commonality in these criteria is that they are all examples of competitive or individual reward structures. That is, these criteria are determined either comparatively, where students are in competition for a limited amount of praise or a limited number of satisfactory grades, or they are determined on some scale that is either absolute or relative to the student's own performance. The reward structure of the majority of classrooms is a competitive one, in which students compete for a necessarily limited number of acceptable grades.

The Traditional Classroom

The traditional classroom may be characterized as consisting of an independent or individualistic task structure and a competitive reward structure. These particular task and reward structures have many virtues. They tend to be easily administered; they are "fair," in that an individual's rewards depend almost entirely on his or her performance (however defined); and they are easily understood by children, parents, and school personnel. However, these traditional task and reward structures have several faults, such as the following:

- Traditional reward structures are not salient for all students. Because of the competitive nature of traditional rewards, many low performing students have little, if any, chance to make acceptable grades, regardless of their effort.
- Traditional reward structures "set students against one another," and, in turn, set many students against academic performance. Because the academic success of one student entails a decrease in the chance that another student will be able to make an acceptable grade, a competitive reward structure disrupts interpersonal bonds among students. Students combat this tendency by discouraging academic performance on

Operational Description

the part of their peers, in the same way that employees in industry express their disapproval of co-workers who work "too hard," thereby making other workers look like laggards. This sets up a situation in which anti-academic peer norms oppose institutional norms, and many students who could achieve at a high level turn their attention to more peer-supported activities, such as sports (see Coleman, 1960).

- Traditional task structures provide few opportunities for active learning. For example, in a class discussion involving 30 students, each student gets an average of only about 1/30th of the time set aside for student responses. In practice, this time is unevenly distributed, with bright, articulate students—those who need the *least* help—taking *most* of the time. For most students, considerable class time is spent in either passive listening or in individual desk work for which feedback may be far removed in time from performance.

Alternative Classroom Modes

An alternative to the individual task is the group task; alternatives to competitive reward structures are individual reward structures and cooperative reward structures.

A group task is one in which students are permitted or encouraged to aid each other in their learning activities. Peer tutoring is one widely used example of a group task, as are various group projects and discussion groups.

There are three possible categories of reward structures: competitive, individual, and cooperative. In a competitive reward structure, there is a limited number of rewards for which students must compete as individuals. Grading on the curve is an example of a competitive reward structure. In an individual reward structure, objective standards of performance are set which make the rewards that an individual receives completely independent of the rewards that others receive (such as in Individually Prescribed Instruction classrooms). Competitive and individual reward structures are most often used in the traditional classroom.

In a cooperative reward structure, rewards are given to groups of students based on the performance of the entire group. Cooperative reward structures may be further divided into group contingencies, in which an objective standard is set for the group to achieve, and group competition, in which groups compete with each other for a limited supply of rewards. Cooperative reward structures, whether they are group contingencies or group competition, have several advantages over individual competition. First, they should motivate all students equally well (Slavin, 1977a). An extra point contributed to a team score is just as useful coming from a low achiever as from a high achiever. Second, they reverse the process inherent in competitive reward structures in which students are "set against" each other and come to oppose academic efforts on the part of their peers. In a cooperative reward structure, the effective performance of a student improves the chances that others will be rewarded. As a result, academically effective students gain in sociometric status in a cooperative reward structure, but lose status in either a competitive reward structure (Slavin, DeVries, and Hulten, 1975) or an individual structure (Slavin, 1977b). Further, cooperative reward structures motivate students to help each other with their academic work (Buckholdt and Wodarski, 1974; DeVries and Edwards, 1973; Edwards and DeVries, 1974; Slavin, 1977b; Wodarski, Hamblin, Buckholdt, and Ferritor, 1973).

In addition to improving achievement, cooperative reward structures have had strong and consistent positive impacts on the social-connectedness of students, such as liking and mutual concern (see Johnson and Johnson, 1974, or Slavin,

1977a, for reviews). For many of the social scientists who have worked on cooperative reward structures, this has been the most important outcome. Some have developed strong ideological commitments to the use of cooperative reward structures in classrooms regardless of their effects on academic performance. The reason for this is not difficult to understand. Cooperative structuring of classrooms could be expected to have long-term, positive effects on the social-connectedness, self-esteem, and possibly general mental health of children. These outcomes have been frequently observed in short-term uses of such structures. However, unless the objectives of schooling are radically redefined, academic performance must be a first priority.

Fostering Learning in Cooperative Groups

Cooperative reward structures must be carefully structured if they are to have positive effects on academic performance. First, they must be designed so that no individuals can "drag their feet" and let the rest of the group do the work. That is, each group member must be individually accountable to the group for his or her behavior. Second, the group task must be one in which the participation of all group members is necessary. A frequently used group reward and task structure that does not meet this criterion is the "group report," in which several students are expected to write one paper. Unless the work is carefully divided, this becomes an essentially individual task, often conducted by the most diligent and academically skilled group member. Third, the group must be rewarded at the group level for a group performance. If students are asked to work together but are evaluated and rewarded only as individuals, there is no group reward structure, and most of the outcomes associated with group reward structures will not occur. Fourth, the group must be rewarded as a group frequently.

These four conditions are bare essentials if a cooperative reward structure is to have positive effects on academic performance. Even if they are met, such outcomes are not guaranteed. Such factors as task structure, team size, magnitude of reward, method of assigning students to teams, etc., are certainly involved. Social science research has only scratched the surface in understanding the dynamics and requirements of cooperative learning groups, but it has nonetheless shown such positive characteristics of learning teams that these interventions cannot be ignored (Johnson and Johnson, 1974).

One important fact frequently forgotten in research on learning groups is that the desirable outcome of schooling is not a product produced by the students themselves. Many studies have investigated "group productivity" (such as number of ideas produced by the group) instead of individual learning, and team learning procedures have been devised to maximize group productivity rather than individual learning. A laboratory group may produce a good report, but has every participant (including those who may have done little to help prepare the report) really learned anything about science? It is the learning, not the quality of the report, that is the important outcome of the task. While group productivity may be increased by means of a variety of informal methods, individual learning is hard work. Students do not automatically possess the level of cooperative skills required to do this work. Cooperative reward structures used in classrooms must be designed so that students are motivated to teach each other and to learn themselves—to do the hard and often painful work of mastering academic material.

It is known that cooperative reward structures have positive effects on students' social-connectedness, attitudes, and possibly mental health, and that they can have positive effects on academic performance under certain conditions. The job is to find those conditions and to create practical interventions to permit the implementation of cooperative reward structures in classrooms.

Teams-Games-Tournament (TGT) is an instructional method which uses what is known about small groups and academic motivation. TGT is capable of producing positive outcomes on social, attitudinal, and academic performance dimensions. It is both a practical program designed for use in typical classrooms, without great expenditure or effort, and a useful research tool with which group processes, peer norms, student attitudes, and academic motivation may be studied by means of experimental manipulations in natural classroom settings. What follows is a description of the TGT structure.

Research has shown that if a cooperative reward/group task system could be constructed to increase student academic performance, other important outcomes (such as increased social-connectedness, pro-academic peer norms, and greater satisfaction with school) could also be anticipated. However, it is also apparent that simply setting up a cooperative reward structure with group tasks will not guarantee positive effects on academic performance. TGT was created with the objective of increasing academic achievement for all children, particularly children who have difficulty under traditional reward and task systems. It was designed with several features critical to the use of a cooperative reward structure and a group task in increasing academic performance.

TGT Features

1. *Small teams.* Research on group size has indicated that small, face-to-face teams are more efficient and cohesive than larger teams (Lott and Lott, 1965).

2. *Heterogeneous teams.* Since a major purpose of the teams is to provide an opportunity for peer tutoring, each team must have a mix of students.

3. *Performance at the individual level.* Most school tasks do not lend themselves naturally to true cooperation or division of labor, particularly as the outcome of education is not a *group* product but is knowledge instilled in *each* student. If learning is to occur in a team reward structure, each student must be individually responsible for his or her performance, and that performance must be evaluated in a setting in which help from teammates is not permitted. Otherwise, responsibility for the group performance will be left with the most able group members, while the less able members are ignored.

4. *Team incentives must be sufficient to motivate team performance and must be delivered frequently.* If teams are to work effectively, they must be motivated to do so. The amount of incentive needed to motivate team performance varies from situation to situation. However, one useful incentive is to have teams engage in team competition, and then to recognize successful teams. This approach avoids the use of (1) grades, which cannot be given at the team level, and (2) material rewards, which are expensive as well as disliked by many teachers and parents. Teams must be rewarded frequently for two reasons. First, frequent rewards are known to be more powerful than infrequent ones in motivating behavior. Second, because students are ultimately evaluated at the individual level instead of the team level, team rewards must be separated from individual evaluations. This can be best accomplished by giving team rewards frequently, while giving individual evaluations less frequently.

5. *The contributions of team members must be equally valuable.* If some students' contributions to the group product are more valued than others' contributions, the less valued students may fail to contribute to their full potential.

TGT Components

TGT, or Teams-Games-Tournament, was designed to be easy for teachers to use, involving minimal expense and only minor additional preparation. A TGT teacher's manual lays out the TGT activities in a step-by-step fashion. The principal components of TGT are as follows:

Teams. Students are assigned by the teacher to four- or five-member teams. Each team reflects a cross-section of the academic ability, race, and sex composition of the class. The teacher ranks the students from top to bottom on past academic performance in the skill area to be taught and then forms teams which contain a high achiever, a low achiever, and two to three average achievers. The teams are balanced on race and sex composition. Team membership remains constant over the course of the TGT instructional period (six to ten weeks). Teammates are usually assigned adjacent seats for that period of time.

Games. Students compete against members of other teams on simple, course content-relevant academic games. These games typically consist of short-answer questions covering material taught in class. Several TGT game sets are being published, and teachers can make their own. The games are played according to a standard set of rules called the General Instructional Game Structure, or GIGS (see Figure 2). A sample TGT game is presented in Appendix A.

Tournaments. Students play the games in frequently-held tournaments. Each tournament takes approximately 40 minutes. They may be held either once or twice per week, depending on the curriculum and the teacher's preferences. In the tournaments, students compete as individuals to contribute points to their teams. They play at three-person, ability-homogeneous "tournament tables." At the conclusion of play at each table, the high scorer brings six points each to his or her team; the middle scorer brings four points; and the low scorer brings two points. This scoring system means that each student, regardless of prior performance level, has a roughly equal chance (one chance in three) of bringing six points to his or her team. Students are assigned to their initial tournament tables based on their achievement rank—the top three students compete at Table No. 1, the next three at Table No. 2, and so on. However, table assignment changes from tournament to tournament.

Bumping. "Bumping" is a procedure used in TGT to assign students to tournament tables after the first tournament. Its purpose is to change competitors to keep interest high and to maintain equal competition at each tournament table. After each tournament, the teacher assigns the high scorer at each tournament table to the next higher table (with higher performing students), the low scorer to the next lower table, and the middle scorer to the same table he or she competed at before. That is, the winner at Table No. 4 is "bumped" to Table No. 3 for the next tournament, the low scorer is "bumped" to Table No. 5, and the middle scorer remains at Table No. 4.

Team Practice. On the day before each tournament, each team is given an opportunity to learn the material to be used in the games. Team members may study together or fill out worksheets, which may either contain the exact game items or a larger set of items from which the game items will be selected. Peer tutoring is encouraged but not required during the team practice sessions.

Newsletters. At the end of each week during which TGT is used, the teacher prepares a dittoed class newsletter and distributes it to the class. The newsletter announces team standings and recognizes individuals who have contributed six points (the maximum) to their team scores. The newsletter can be taken home by students and is usually posted around the class to provide maximum recognition for the teams and students who have done well. A sample newsletter is presented in Appendix B.

In using TGT in the classroom, teachers typically follow one of two weekly schedules presented in the TGT manual. One schedule involves three periods of traditional teaching, followed by one period of team practice, and one period of tournament (usually held on a Friday). An alternative schedule involves a more intensive use of TGT, with two tournaments and two team practice sessions per week.

References

Buckholdt, D. R., and Wodarski, J. S. *The Effects of Different Reinforcement Systems on Cooperative Behaviors Exhibited by Children in Classroom Contexts.* Paper presented at the Annual Meeting of the American Psychological Association, New Orleans, 1974.

Coleman, J. S. The Adolescent Subculture and Academic Achievement. *American Journal of Sociology*, 1960, *65*, 337-347.

DeVries, D. L., and Edwards, K. J. Learning Games and Student Teams: Their Effects on Classroom Process. *American Educational Research Journal*, 1973, *10*, 307-318.

Edwards, K. J., and DeVries, D. L. *The Effects of Teams-Games-Tournament and Two Structural Variations on Classroom Process, Student Attitudes, and Student Achievement.* Center for Social Organization of Schools, Johns Hopkins University, 1974, Report No. 172.

Johnson, D. W., and Johnson, R. T. Instructional Goal Structure: Cooperative, Competitive, or Individualistic? *Review of Educational Research*, 1974, *44*, 213-240.

Lott, A. J., and Lott, B. E. Group Cohesiveness as Interpersonal Attraction: A Review of Relationships with Antecedent and Consequent Variables. *Psychological Bulletin,* 1965, *64,* 259-309.

Slavin, R.E. Classroom Reward Structure: An Analytic and Practical Review. *Review of Educational Research,* 1977, *47,* 633-650. (a)

Slavin, R.E. A Student Team Approach to Teaching Adolescents with Special Emotional and Behavioral Needs. *Psychology in the Schools,* 1977, *14,* 77-84. (b)

Slavin, R.E., DeVries, D.L., and Hulten, B.H. *Individual vs. Team Competition: The Interpersonal Consequences of Academic Performance.* Center for Social Organization of Schools, Johns Hopkins University, 1975, Report No. 188.

Wodarski, J.S., Hamblin, R.L., Buckholdt, D., and Ferritor, D.E. Individual Consequences vs. Different Shared Consequences Contingent on the Performance of Low-Achieving Group Members. *Journal of Applied Social Psychology,* 1973, *3,* 276-290.

III.

DESIGN FORMAT

Getting Ready to Use TGT

The decisions and preparations you should make before you teach your first lesson with TGT are outlined below and described in detail in the following pages.

Step 1: Initial Decisions to Be Made
—Is TGT suitable for your grade?
—With what subject will you use TGT?
—With what class will you use TGT?
—At what point in the unit will you introduce TGT?

Step 2: Making Up the Teams
—Rank order the students in the class.
—Decide how many teams you will have.
—Assign students to teams.
—Make a master list of the teams and their members.

Step 3: Preparing Worksheets and Games
—Decide if you will use prepared worksheets and games or make your own.
—Reproduce materials.
—Play the game yourself.

Step 4: Preparing the Tournament Materials
—Game Score Sheets
—Tournament Score Sheets
—Team Summary Sheets

Step 1: Initial Decisions to Be Made
  —Is TGT suitable for your grade?
  —With what subject will you use TGT?
  —With what class will you use TGT?
  —At what point in the unit will you introduce TGT?

Is TGT suitable for your grade? TGT can be used with any group of students, with the exception of very young children. Although it is possible to use one or two of TGT's basic elements successfully with very young children, the combination is less effective at these levels because the students have usually not had prior experience with cooperative group work and team competition in academic subjects. Generally, by the time students begin the third grade, they have had these experiences and are able to understand the relationship between TGT's elements. As to the highest grade level for which TGT is appropriate, college students have been successfully involved in the technique, and it is conceivable that TGT could be effective in adult education classes.

With what subject will you use TGT? TGT can be used with any subject—whether it be language arts, social studies, mathematics, science, or physical education (see Appendix A for sample games). However, until you become acquainted with the procedures, you should probably use TGT with only one subject. Research has shown that TGT can help students become more interested in a subject. Therefore, if you teach several subjects to the same class of students, you might try TGT first with the subject that most of your students find least interesting. These tend to be subjects which require repetitive exposure to a few basic skills. For example, a seventh grade math course concentrating on multiplication and division operations would be appropriate.

With what class will you use TGT? If you teach more than one class of students, you should probably use TGT in only one of your classes until you have some experience with the routines. Because research results suggest that TGT develops positive relationships among students and between students and their teachers, you might want to use TGT first with the class that needs the most help in developing positive, interpersonal relationships. Also, because effective student teams require a range of abilities among the teammates, the class should not be "tracked," but should instead include a range of ability levels.

At what point in the unit will you introduce TGT? It is generally a good practice to introduce TGT after a unit of work is underway. Thus, the students will be somewhat knowledgeable about the concepts and skills they will be required to use and will be better able to concentrate on learning how TGT operates. Once your students know how TGT operates, it is wise to incorporate TGT into all phases of a teaching unit. If incorporated early into subsequent teaching units, TGT can give students an important incentive for acquiring the skills to be taught in the new unit.

Step 2: Making Up the Teams
—Rank order the students in the class.
—Decide how many teams you will have.
—Assign students to teams.
—Make a master list of the teams and their members.

Rank order the students in the class. From the highest to the lowest, rank the students in the class according to their achievement, or performance, in the subject with which you will use TGT. (*Note*: Achievement implies performance in the class; it does not refer to an IQ score or a standardized achievement test score.) If the class has been meeting for some time, a numerical score which summarizes all previous performance (e.g., quizzes, homework) in the class could be formed for each student. Then, copy the names of the students onto a sheet of paper. List the highest-achieving student's name first, then the second highest-achieving student, and so forth, until you have ordered each student's name by rank in the class. Make it as exact as possible but realize that the middle will be difficult to differentiate. For example, if two students are tied for 15th place, you can arbitrarily place one in 15th place and one in 16th place.

Decide how many teams you will have. Each team should have four members. To decide how many teams you will have, divide the number of students in the class by four. If the division is even, the quotient will be the number of four-member teams you will have. For example, if there are 32 students in the class, you would have eight teams with four members each.

If the division is uneven, and the remainder is one, two, or three, then you have one, two, or three teams composed of five members. For example, if there are 30 students in the class, you would have a total of seven teams. Five of these teams would have four members each, and two of these teams would have five members each.

Assign students to teams. When you are assigning the students to teams, you must balance the teams so that (1) each team is composed of students whose achievement levels range from low-to-average-to-high, and (2) the average achievement level of all the teams in the class is about equal. There are two reasons for this. First, by having low, average, and high achievement levels within the team, students can tutor each other and have more meaningful team practice sessions. Second, by having the average achievement level across teams equivalent, no team has an advantage in the tournament competition.

To achieve this balance within and across teams, the teams should be composed as follows. Four-member teams should have one high-achieving student, two average-achieving students, and one low-achieving student. Five-member teams

Design Format

should have one high-achieving student, three average-achieving students, and one low-achieving student.

In addition to balancing the teams by achievement levels of the members, you should also balance the teams in terms of sex and race. Although sex and race balancing are desirable, whether or not they take priority over achievement balancing depends upon your reasons for using TGT. However, because there may be several students within each of the achievement groups whose performance is roughly comparable, you should be able to make slight adjustments to avoid having teams composed entirely of students of the same sex. And, in racially integrated classes, you should also make adjustments to avoid having teams composed entirely of students whose race is in the minority in the class. The reason for this is to facilitate interaction, especially in the practice sessions of the teams, between students of opposite sex and different races.

If all the teams in your class will have four members (i.e., the number of students is divided evenly by four), then you could assign the students to teams as shown in Figure 1. In the example, the class has 32 students. This means that there will be a total of eight teams (Teams A-H), each with four members.

In order to assure that each team has a range of achievement levels and that the average achievement level is equal across teams, the first eight students are assigned to each of the eight teams in descending order. Then, the last eight students are assigned to each of the eight teams in ascending order. Finally, the average-achieving students are assigned. To assign the average-achieving students, the class median is located. This is between Student #16 and Student #17. Starting with these two students, the average-achieving students are assigned in ascending and descending order from the class median to the eight teams.

Thus, each team has one high-achieving student, two average-achieving students, and one low-achieving student. To

Figure 1

	Rank Order	Team Name
High-Achieving Students	1 2 3 4 5 6 7 8	A B C D E F G H
Average-Achieving Students	9 10 11 12 13 14 15 16 17 18 19 20 21 22 23 24	H G F E D C B A A B C D E F G H
Low-Achieving Students	25 26 27 28 29 30 31 32	H G F E D C B A

Design Format

make the average achievement level of each team as even as possible, the assigned students "balance" each other. For example, Team A is assigned the highest-achieving student (Student #1) and the lowest-achieving student (Student #32), whose class performance should balance to an "average." Team A is also assigned the two students who are on either side of the class median (Students #16 and #17) and are the average students in the class. Team H, on the other hand, is assigned the lowest high-achieving student (Student #8) who is balanced by the highest low-achieving student (Student #25). From the average-achieving group, Team H is assigned the highest average-achieving student (Student #9) and the lowest average-achieving student (Student #24).

As a check, to verify that the ranks of the students assigned to each team are indeed comparable, simply average the team members' ranks within the ordered list. For example:

$$\text{Team A: } 1 + 16 + 17 + 32 = 66/4 = 16.5$$
$$\text{Team B: } 2 + 15 + 18 + 31 = 66/4 = 16.5$$
$$\text{Team C: } 3 + 14 + 19 + 30 = 66/4 = 16.5$$
$$\text{Team D: } 4 + 13 + 20 + 29 = 66/4 = 16.5$$
$$\text{Team E: } 5 + 12 + 21 + 28 = 66/4 = 16.5$$
$$\text{Team F: } 6 + 11 + 22 + 27 = 66/4 = 16.5$$
$$\text{Team G: } 7 + 10 + 23 + 26 = 66/4 = 16.5$$
$$\text{Team H: } 8 + 9 + 24 + 25 = 66/4 = 16.5$$

However, as mentioned previously, you should make some adjustments in the students' rank order to avoid having teams that are all of the same sex or, in racially integrated classes, of the minority race. This adjustment should be made when you assign the average-achieving students. Thus, for the example illustrated above, if Student #1 is a black female and Student #23 is a white female, when assigning the average-achieving students an attempt would be made to balance the team by sex. If possible, two males (preferably a black male and a white male) would be assigned from the average-achieving group of students. But an attempt also would be made to make sure that the average-achieving students so assigned are ranked close to positions #16 and #17 on the class list.

If some of the teams in your class have five members (i.e., the number of students is not evenly divisible by four), you can assign students in basically the same way as outlined in Figure 1. The only difference will involve a surplus of students at the middle-achieving ranks. Minor changes in team membership can be made at this level without changing the overall comparability of the teams.

The assignment of students to teams described above suggests an exactness which (1) is not achievable in many classes, and (2) ignores other things, such as maturity of the teammates, which may be critical in determining a team's success. For this reason, teams can be viewed as having equal resources even though the sums of members' ranks are not equivalent. For example, for teams having an average of 16 for the members' ranks, any team within a range of plus or minus two points (14 to 18) could be considered equivalent.

Many teachers who use teams allow the students to form their own teams along friendship lines. Although this procedure may immediately create cohesive teams in your class, it does not necessarily result in hard-working teams. In addition, such groups are often chosen along racial or sex lines (since students choose as friends other students very much like themselves). When such homogeneous teams compete, the natural social barriers which already exist in classrooms become rigidified. Consequently, you should not use friendship choices as a basis for creating anything but the most *ad hoc*, or temporary, teams.

Make a master list of the teams and their members. After you have finished assigning students to teams, make a list of the names of the students and their team assignments. You should make this list now, while you are working on the team assignments. You will need to use the list when you inform the students of their team assignments.

Design Format

Step 3: Preparing Worksheets and Games
—Decide if you will use prepared worksheets and games or make your own.
—Reproduce materials.
—Play the game yourself.

Decide if you will use prepared worksheets and games or make your own. For each TGT unit, you will need a worksheet that lets students practice the skills they will need to do well in the game and a set of items to use in the game that parallels the worksheet items. Inexpensive worksheets and games in mathematics for grades 2-8, language mechanics for grades 3-8, and elementary and high school nutrition are currently available from the Johns Hopkins Team Learning Project, 3505 N. Charles St., Baltimore, MD 21218. Other materials, in language arts (grades 4-9), vocabulary (grades 4-6), and verbal analogies (grades 4-6), can be obtained from Argus Communications, Niles, Illinois 60648. The Johns Hopkins materials consist of single copies of worksheets and game sheets that must be duplicated, while the Argus worksheets are on ditto masters and the game items are on cards. These prepared materials make it easy to use TGT. If you wish to use TGT in a subject not covered by these materials, or if you wish to more closely customize your materials to your own curriculum, you should make your own worksheets and games. Figure 2 summarizes the steps you need to follow to make your own worksheets and games.

The games that you make are used with GIGS (General Instructional Game Structure), which is a set of playing rules and procedures. (See Figure 3.) Thus, you can vary the content of each successive game, but the rules for playing each game stay the same and students do not need to learn new rules. Appendix A contains samples of two games based on GIGS.

Reproduce Materials. In the tournament, students play the game in groups of three players.

Each team should have two worksheets to study. Giving each team only two worksheets helps to emphasize the idea that students should work with their teammates, not simply fill out and hand in their worksheets. It also emphasizes the idea that the worksheets are study aids, not quizzes or worksheets to be done once and handed in whether or not the students understand them. Therefore, you will need to reproduce one worksheet and worksheet answer sheet for every two students, for example, 16 in a class of 32. If after a few weeks your teams are working well together and understand that the worksheets are study aids, you may give each student his or her own worksheet.

Play the game yourself. Before you introduce and use GIGS (see Figure 3) with your students, you should play the game yourself with your family or friends. You will gain a working acquaintance with the game materials and sequence of play, and you will be sensitive to unclear directions or situations for which you may have to interpret or supply a rule when the game is played by your students. Cheating is very difficult to do in a three-person GIGS game, because two competitors are always watching the third. However, playing the game yourself will prepare you for the kinds of things some of your students might try, and it will enable you to watch for and hopefully prevent them.

Step 4: Preparing the Tournament Materials
—Game Score Sheets
—Tournament Score Sheets
—Team Summary Sheets

Game score sheets. The game score sheets are used to record the scores of the players during the tournament sessions. Each table receives a game score sheet. The game score sheet should include a line for the date, the class identification number or name, the tournament table number, the round number, the players' names and teams, and the players' scores. Because a playing group may be able to complete

Design Format

Figure 2

Making Worksheets and Games

Making worksheets and games for TGT is no different from making good worksheets and quizzes for traditional instruction. A worksheet consists of 20-40 items on the objective you are teaching. The items can be fill-in-the-blank, multiple-choice, or any format you desire. These items should be numbered and typed or written on a ditto sheet. A worksheet answer sheet must also be typed or written on a separate ditto sheet. The game consists of items that should be parallel to the worksheet items. That is, the game items should get at the same concept and be of the same difficulty as the worksheet items. If the skill being taught requires memorization, the items should be the same on both. For example, parallel pairs of items are listed below.

Worksheet	**Game**
1. $1/2 + 1/6 =$ _____	1. $1/4 + 3/8 =$ _____
2. My dog barks it is brown. Fragment complete run-on	2. New York is a great, big, beautiful city. Fragment complete run-on
3. What is the plural of *ox*? _____	3. What is the plural of *ox*? _____

Note that Item #3 is repeated in the game because the plural of "ox" does not follow a rule, but must be memorized. In the other two cases it is a concept or operation that is being taught, so the actual items are different.

The game should have the same number of items as the worksheet, and the game items and a game answer sheet must be numbered and put on ditto masters.

If you make your own materials, you will also need to make decks of number cards. These can be obtained from the Johns Hopkins Team Learning Project, or you can make them yourself. You will need one

(Continued on Next Page)

Figure 2 (Continued)

deck of cards numbered 1-40 for every three students in your class. The cards should be on heavy paper cut to playing-card size.

Sample worksheets and games for TGT are reproduced in Appendix A. Further instructions for making TGT units appear in Chapter V and in Figures 13-15.

Figure 3

GIGS: General Instructional Game Structure

MATERIALS NEEDED: (1) Number cards
                                  (2) Game sheet
                                  (3) Answer sheet
                                  (4) Game score sheet

The Rules

1. To start the game, shuffle the deck of number cards and place it face down on the table. Also place the answer sheet face down on the table. Decide who will be player number 1. Play proceeds in a clockwise direction from player number 1.

2. Each player, in turn, takes the top card from the deck, reads the item corresponding to that number aloud, and does either a. or b. below:

    a. States that he or she does not know the answer and asks if another player wants to give an answer. If no one answers, the card is placed on the bottom of the deck. If another player gives an answer, he or she follows the procedure described under alternative b.

    b. Answers the question immediately and asks if anyone wants to challenge the answer. The player to the left of the person giving the answer has the right to challenge first and give a different answer. If he or she passes, the next player to the left can challenge.

3. When there is no challenge, the player to the right checks the answer:

    a. If the answer is correct, the player keeps the card.

    b. If the answer is wrong, the player puts the card on the bottom of the deck.

4. When there is a challenge and the challenger gives an answer:

    a. If the answer is correct, the challenger receives the card.

    b. If the challenger is incorrect and the original answer is correct, the challenger must give up one of his or her other cards, if any, and place it on the bottom of the deck.

(Continued on Next Page)

Figure 3 (Continued)

    c. If both the challenger's answer and the original answer are wrong, only the card in play is placed on the bottom of the deck.

5. The game ends when there are no more cards in the deck. Each player counts up the number of cards he or she has and records this number as the score on the game score sheet. The player with the most cards is the winner.

Design Format

more than one play of the game in one session, the game score sheet should provide spaces to record the scores of three to five games, as well as the total score for the session.

A copy of the game score sheet is reproduced in Figure 4.

When you are preparing the ditto master for the game score sheet, you can probably place two or three sheets on one ditto master. This will make it easier to duplicate a large quantity of game score sheets inexpensively.

Tournament score sheets. The tournament score sheet is used to record the total game scores for each student in the class and to note the number of tournament points a player's total game score equals. This sheet will also make it easier for you to assign students to tables for the next tournament session.

A copy (of the first few lines) of a tournament score sheet is reproduced in Figure 5. When you make the ditto master for your class, be sure to include one line for each student in the class. You will need one tournament score sheet for each tournament session.

Team summary sheets. The team summary sheets provide a record of the weekly tournament points for each member of the team, the team's weekly total, and the individual and team points cumulated to date. This information is used to prepare the weekly newsletter that is distributed to the class the day following the tournament session. A copy of the team summary sheet is reproduced in Figure 6. You will need one for each team.

Guide to Daily Lessons

The First Week

The first week's lessons are sequenced to introduce each of TGT's three basic elements separately. This gives the students a chance to learn how to play the game, how the tournament

Figure 4

Game Score Sheet							
Date .... Class							
Tournament Table # .... Round #							

PLAYERS		SCORES					
Names	Team	Game 1	Game 2	Game 3	Game 4	Game 5	DAY'S TOTAL
1.							
2.							
3.							
4.							
5.							

Figure 5

Table #	Players' Names	Team Name	Game Score Day's Total	Tournament Points	Table Assignment For Next Round

Tournament Score Sheet

Date .... Round # ....

is structured, and how to work in small groups without requiring them to absorb the relationship between the basic elements at the outset. Once the students become familiar with the procedures and the materials used in each of the three activities, they will be better able to understand the nature of TGT as a whole. Also, it allows you to correct any misunderstandings and to identify any problems the students seem to be having with one of the three activities. If all three were introduced simultaneously, it would be more difficult to identify the source of a problem and correct it.

The suggested sequence of lessons (see Figure 7) assumes that you and your students will move fairly quickly through the introductory activities. However, you are the best person to judge the pace of the activities for your students. Therefore, if it is too slow or too fast, you should adjust the suggested schedule accordingly.

Day 1: Introduce the Game

Lesson Background

The *purpose* of this lesson is teaching the students how to play the game. The lesson should take one class period and include the following activities: explaining the purpose of the game to be played, and playing as well as scoring the game. As to *materials* needed, only copies of the game will be required (remember you will need one copy for each of the three-person tables).

Instructions for the Lesson

1. *Set up the game.* Before beginning the game session, you should: arrange the desks to form three-member playing tables; set game materials on each table; and ask the students to sit at one of the tables.

2. *Introduce the game to players.* Explain the purpose and

Design Format

Figure 6

Team Summary Sheet

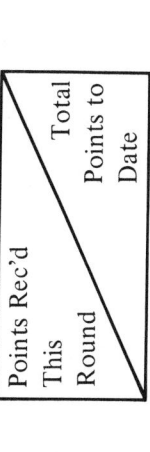

rules of the game. In explaining the rules, you might use a hypothetical group, examining each step of the game.

3. *Play the game.* All students should play the game once. While they are playing the game, move from group to group, watching for confusion concerning the rules. After the students have completed the game, show the students how to calculate their final score.

Day 2: Review Lesson

The *purpose* of this lesson is to review (1) the concepts or skills being used in the game, and (2) the game itself. You might begin the lesson using items from the game (which students clearly had not mastered) as examples of important concepts or skills yet to be learned. Conclude the lesson by having the students play the game.

Day 3: Practice Tournament I

Lesson Background

The *purpose* of this lesson is to introduce the tournament structure to the students. Because the students will not be competing in this tournament as representatives of their teams, you should avoid using the word "team" in this tournament. The team competition component will be taught later. *Materials* required for this period are tournament table markers, game score sheets, copies of the game, and a rank order list of the students.

Instructions for the Lesson

1. *Assign the students to tournament tables.* After the class has started, assign the students to tournament tables as follows. Using the list of students by rank order, assign the first three students to Tournament Table No. 1, the next three to Tournament Table No. 2, and so forth until all of the students have been assigned to a tournament table. If necessary,

Figure 7

Suggested Sequence for the First Week

Day 1	Day 2	Day 3	Day 4	Day 5
Introduce the game	Review Lesson —review skills required in game —review game	Practice Tournament I	Team Practice Session	Practice Tournament II

create one or two tables with two or four students.

2. *Introduce the tournament to the students.* In your introduction, you might say the following:

> Over the next several weeks, we will be playing a tournament in this class. Each of you will be assigned to a tournament table, where you will compete against two other students. Sometimes, you may be competing against only one other student, or you may be competing against three other students.
>
> During the tournament, you will play a game, similar to the game we have been playing for the past two days. In today's Practice Tournament, you will play that same game again.
>
> Today, we will try to play two, and possibly three, rounds of the tournament. When most of the groups have finished playing the game, I will call time. Then, we will add up the scores and see which players will move.

3. *Play the tournament.* At the end of the first game (allow about 15 minutes), have the students complete one of the game score sheets, shuffle the cards, and continue with a second game.

At the end of the second game, follow the same procedure as above. If there is insufficient time for a third round of the tournament, have the students begin another game at the same tournament table.

If a student is late for the start of the tournament, assign the student to a table where he or she will be competing against students with a comparable achievement level. This may mean placing the student at a table where there are already three players, but it is better to do this than to assign the student to a table where he or she would have a great advantage or disadvantage with respect to the other players who were initially assigned to that table.

4. *Collect the game score sheets.* Make sure you have a completed game score sheet from each table for each round that was played during the period.

Design Format 43

Day 4: Team Practice Session

Lesson Background

The *purpose* of this lesson is to have the students work in small groups. Such small-group work is important because (1) it gives students the opportunity to tutor their peers, and (2) it allows for a structured practice time for the tournament that will be held on Day 5.

The *materials* required are (1) a list of teams (duplicate one copy for each student), (2) a worksheet (one copy per student), and (3) copies of the game. The worksheet can be of any format but should contain items similar to those on the game and should be related to the curriculum unit under study.

Instructions for the Lesson

1. *Set up the classroom.* Since the students will be working in groups of four, for the most part, arrange the desks in the classroom to accommodate four students. You might want to consider assigning the teammates permanent seats that are adjacent; this will facilitate their interacting and helping one another with assignments other than those that come on the Team Practice Session days.

2. *Introduce the students to the idea of teams.* In your introduction, you might say the following:

> Over the next several weeks, while we are playing the tournament in this class, you will compete with the other students as a representative of a team. Yesterday, when we played the tournament, you competed as an individual. When we play again, and you compete as a representative of your team, your score will be used to determine how many tournament points you earned during the round. These tournament points will be added to the points the other members of your team earned to get a team score. All the winners at a table will receive the same number of points, all the middle scorers the same number of points, and all the losers the same number of points. Everyone will receive

some points; no one will receive a zero. So, it may be possible for all the members of a team to earn the same number of points. If, for example, each member of your team was a winner at his or her tournament table, then your team would have a high score for the day.

Every week the teams will have a chance to work together to practice and help each other get ready for the tournament. Today, I am going to assign you to teams. Then, you will have some time to work together as a team and prepare for the tournament that will be held tomorrow.

3. *Assign the students to their teams.* Distribute the duplicated copies of the list of teams.

4. *Assign the teams to seats.* Tell the teams where they should sit.

5. *Distribute the worksheets and tell the students what they should do.* When you distribute the worksheets, you should make certain that you mention how the groups are to work together and how the task is related to the game. For example, you might want the students to complete the worksheet independently, and then discuss their answers with their teammates. You might want the students to divide the responsibility for completing the task. You simply might want the students to complete the assignment as a group. Whatever procedure you recommend, make sure that the teammates will have an opportunity to work together at some point and to be either a "teacher" or a "learner" at some point during the period.

6. *Work with individual students or individual teams.* While the teams are working on the worksheet, you should circulate about the classroom. Give the teams assistance in starting the assignment. Then, take this opportunity to work with students whom you know could benefit from individualized instruction. Also, since students are usually not used to working together, you should encourage specific high-achieving students who are not helping their teammates to do so.

Preparation Required Between Day 4 and Day 5

Assign Students to Tournament Tables

On Day 5, Practice Tournament II, the students will compete as representatives of their team. In preparation for this tournament, you should assign students to tournament tables. During the game competition, teams do not compete as teams. Rather, each team member is assigned to a tournament table to compete against two students who represent other teams. At a given table, the three students should be roughly matched on achievement level. Such matching gives each student a reasonable chance of succeeding at the game tasks.

The student, competing against only two classmates, no longer feels that he or she is competing against the entire class. In addition, the chance that each student will be positively reinforced (i.e., succeed at the game task) is approximately one-third and is the same for all students. This reinforcement is effective because it immediately follows the appropriate student behavior (i.e., successfully completing an academic task). This is especially true in games based on GIGS; the player learns immediately if he or she has given the correct response. Even if the student does answer incorrectly, this "failure" is not singled out to the entire class and he or she has a chance to give a correct answer the next time.

For the *first* tournament, assign the students to the tournament tables using the rank order listing of the class referred to earlier. Assign the students in the following order: Assign the first three students (ranks 1, 2, and 3) to Tournament Table No. 1, the next three students to Tournament Table No. 2, and so on, until all students are assigned. If the total number of students is not divisible by three, create some tables with two or four players.

Day 5: Practice Tournament II

Purpose of the Lesson

The *purpose* of this lesson is to begin the tournament competition in which team members compete as representatives of their team. It is called a Practice Tournament because the scores will not be used in calculating the season's score for the teams and the team members. The scores from the Practice Round will give the team members some idea of where they stand in relation to the other teams and will give them some incentive to help each other during next week's Team Practice Session.

Time Required for the Lesson
One class period is required.

Materials Required for the Lesson
1. Decks of Number Cards—one for each table
2. Game Score Sheets—one for each table
3. Copies of game and answer sheet—one for each table
4. List of tournament table assignments and directions for assigning team members to tables

Instructions for the Lesson

1. *Set up the tournament tables.* Provide each tournament table with a set of game materials and a game score sheet.

2. *Assign the students to tournament tables.* After the class has started, assign the students to tournament tables according to the assignments you prepared earlier. If a student is absent or late, make adjustments; but make sure that any adjustment places a student at a table where he or she will compete with students of comparable achievement level and who are on different teams. If necessary, create one or two tables with two or four students.

Design Format 47

3. *Introduce the tournament to the students.* In your introduction, you might say the following:

> Today you are going to compete in the tournament as a representative of your team. We will consider this first tournament to be a Practice Round and will not count the scores toward the season's total. However, the scores from today's tournament will be used to determine at what table you will play next week.
>
> Each day on which you play the tournament will be one round in the tournament. You will stay at the same table for the entire period and will play the game as many times as you can. So, if you do not do very well in the first game, you will have a chance to play it again during the period and improve your score for the day. Likewise, if you win the first game, you could lose the next game. So, be careful.
>
> At the end of the period, we will total the points you have received.

4. *Play the practice round.* Have the groups play the game as many times as they can during the period. When the period is almost over, have the players figure out the number of points they have for the game they are playing (if they have not finished). Make sure the players complete the game score sheet at the end of each game.

5. *Calculate game scores and tournament points.* Have the students add up the scores they won in each game and fill in their day's total on the sheet. Have them calculate tournament points as indicated in Figure 8 and fill in the tournament points in the space provided on their game score sheets.

6. *Collect the game score sheets.* Explain to the students that the scores determine how many points they earned for their team.

7. *Figuring team scores.* After you have collected the game score sheets and checked to be sure that the "Day's Total" scores have been correctly transformed to tournament points, you are ready to figure team scores. To do this, simply fill in

the tournament points earned by each team member on the Team Summary Sheet and add to get the total team score. If there are four team members, you are finished. However, if there are three or five team members, you will need to transform the team score to be fair in comparing scores (see Figure 9). For example, if a five-member team receives a total score of 22, the team will receive a transformed score of 18. Only the transformed scores for three- or five-member teams should be considered in determining the team rank. The individual cumulative scores and the cumulative total score the team has made to date are also recorded on the Team Summary Sheet. Of course, it is the transformed scores that are used to get the cumulative team score.

*Assigning the Players to Tables
for the Next Tournament*

Bumping procedure (see Figure 10). The top scorers at each table will be moved up to the next tournament table in the hierarchy; the low scorers at each table will be moved down to the next tournament table; the middle scorers will stay at the same tournament table during the next round of the tournament. To resolve a tie, toss a coin. At Tournament Table No. 1, only the loser moves (down) and at the last tournament table only the winner moves (up). For example, for the three players at Tournament Table No. 3, the top scorer will move up to Tournament Table No. 2; the middle scorer will remain at Tournament Table No. 3; and the low scorer will move down to Tournament Table No. 4.

Before you make any assignments for the next tournament competition, record at the bottom of the Tournament Score Sheet the names of those students who were absent for this week's tournament competition. For the absentees, indicate in the "Table Assignment for Next Round" column the table at which they should have played. Then assign them to the same tables for the next round of the tournament. Then, using the tournament bumping procedure, assign the players to tables for the next round.

It may become necessary for you to make adjustments, since you may have had tables where there were two or four players. When you make the adjustments, make certain that students are assigned to tournament tables that are adjacent to those at which they did play, or should have played. The tournament structure, with bumping, is designed to maintain homogeneous groupings while taking into account new learning. In this way, it compensates for differential learning rates. As the tournament progresses, teammates may be unavoidably assigned to the same table. If, on a given day, such teammates object strongly, you can adjust the bumping procedure to prevent such overlapping.

Prepare the Tournament Newsletter

It is important to relay to the students the results of each tournament in a way which generates interest in the tournament competition. For this purpose a classroom newsletter, or bulletin board, can be most effective. Such newsletters or bulletins should include a summary of the relative performance of both teams and individual students. Appendix B contains a sample newsletter.

Guide to Daily Lessons

The Second and Subsequent Weeks

After the initial introductory lessons have been taught, you will be ready to proceed with TGT and arrange to have certain activities fall on specified days of the week. If you use the model outlined in Figure 11, you will have the weekends to prepare the Tournament Newsletter and make the assignments for the next tournament competition.

In the preceding pages of this chapter, detailed suggestions were given for planning each of the lessons. In this section,

Figure 8

For a Four-Player Game

Player	No. Ties	Tie For Top	Tie For Middle	Tie For Low	3-Way Tie For Top	3-Way Tie For Low	4-Way Tie	Tie For Low and High
Top Scorer	6 points	5	6	6	5	6	4	5
High Middle Scorer	4 points	5	4	4	5	3	4	5
Low Middle Scorer	3 points	3	4	3	5	3	4	3
Low Scorer	2 points	2	2	3	2	3	4	3

For a Three-Player Game

Player	No. Ties	Tie For Top Score	Tie For Low Score	Three-Way Tie
Top Scorer	6 points	5	6	4
Middle Scorer	4 points	5	3	4
Low Scorer	2 points	2	3	4

For a Two-Player Game

Player	No. Ties	Tied
Top Scorer	6 points	4
Low Scorer	2 points	4

Design Format

Figure 9

*Transforming Scores for Teams
with Two, Three, and Five Members*

Raw Score	Two-Member Team	Three-Member Team	Five-Member Team
4	8		
5	10		
6	12	8	
7	14	9	
8	16	11	
9	18	12	
10	20	13	8
11	22	15	9
12	24	16	10
13		17	10
14		19	11
15		20	12
16		21	13
17		23	14
18		24	14
19			15
20			16
21			17
22			18
23			18
24			19
25			20
26			21
27			22
28			22
29			23
30			24

the discussion will be limited to those days on which one of the elements of TGT is a part of the lesson for the day.

Day 2: Playing the Game

When attempting to integrate TGT into your teaching, it is important to view TGT as an ongoing activity which is used periodically throughout a unit of study. In the earlier part of the unit, the game serves as an advance organizer and provides a motivation to learning the material. During the unit, the game functions as a skill drill; and, toward the end of the unit, the game can be used to review and summarize what has been taught.

Day 4: Team Practice Session

Over a period of weeks, the team members will begin to tutor each other in order to improve their tournament score. Teammates, through tutoring, can increase the probability of a player's winning. Peer group pressure channels the behavior of classmates and fosters tutoring. Since the tournament rewards teams as well as individuals, an interdependency is created among team members that demands interaction. The tournament also allows every student to receive positive rewards for contributions to the team effort. It encourages proper scholastic attitudes and behavior. For effective peer tutoring to occur, the Team Practice Session requires your active direction and encouragement. An important part of such direction is assigning specific worksheets on which teams are to work.

After the tournament is underway and the team members have begun to develop a group identification, you may want to suggest that the teams select names for themselves. Teams generally prefer their own original name to Team A, Team B, etc. (see sample newsletter in Appendix B for examples).

Design Format 55

Figure 11

Suggested Sequence
The Second and Subsequent Weeks

Day 1	Day 2	Day 3	Day 4	Day 5
Distribute Newsletters Teach regular lesson	Teach regular lesson Play game	Teach regular lessons	Team Practice Session	Tournament

tournament points for the round and the total points accumulated (or received) to date. After the team summary sheets are completed, it is simply a matter of ordering them twice—once to rank, from highest to lowest, the team scores for the day and once to rank the team scores for the season—and transferring the information to the newsletter.

Ending the Tournament

The tournament should take place over a period of several weeks, preferably a semester. You can end the tournament, however, at any point. When you decide to end the tournament, give the teams at least a week's notice, so that they can try to prepare for the final tournament round and improve their season record.

It may become necessary to have one or more playoffs in order to declare a team or an individual winner for the season. If this is necessary, schedule another round of the tournament and count only the scores of the members of the teams who were tied for first place. If the tie is between players for season's top scorer, then schedule a game where the students who are tied compete with students whose achievement levels are comparable to theirs; or where the tied students compete. Count the scores only of the students who are tied for top scorer—for the other students, the tournament is over. They are only participating in another round of the game to help break the tie.

Problems Within Teams

Most teammates will get along with one another, especially after they have had a couple of weeks to get used to working together. However, some teams will not get along so well, and some students (usually a very small number) will prefer not to work in teams at all.

Whatever you do when problems within teams arise, do not change team assignments except in the most hopeless situations. If students realize that they will be working with a group of students for several weeks, they will almost always learn to get along with them. If they think the teacher might move them to a team with their friends, they might not try so hard. We have seen many teams that looked hopeless at first but finally pulled together and began to work effectively. This improvement takes place most easily when the teacher makes it clear to students that he or she values cooperation and expects the teams to work well together.

If a student cannot get along with his or her team, or prefers to work alone, you may allow the student to work separately but still count his or her score in the team score. In most cases, these students will eventually be able to rejoin their teams if you keep the door open for them to do so.

It is very important that you set a tone of helpfulness, cooperation, and mutual support and that you emphasize that every team member makes a contribution to the team. If the students see that you value cooperation and team success, they will value them too. If your teams do not seem adequately motivated by the class newsletters or bulletin boards, you may add other prizes (such as cookies, free time, or special privileges). These prizes are important to communicate to students that you really do think that working well as a team is important.

Absences

You may make your own decisions about how to handle absences for tournament sessions. If absenteeism is not a problem in your class and you do not wish to penalize absentees, then transform the team score using Figure 9 as though the team were smaller. If you do wish to penalize absentees, give each absentee a minimum score (two points). However, do not use this score in the bumping; try to return the student to the tournament table at which he or she would have played. Absences at times other than the tournament are less of a problem, as the work missed on those days can be made up as usual.

motivator, and evaluator as well as instructor. The TGT structure relieves the teacher of many of these often conflicting roles. The technique provides a classroom organization and a regular format for student work, motivation, and evaluation. This leaves the teacher with an undivided responsibility to provide information to students. Students soon learn that the teacher is a valuable resource for information needed to do well in the TGT competition.

Another important change in the classroom authority structure is a change in the student's role. The student is no longer simply receiving information, but is now made responsible for his or her own learning. Students have a clear-cut task to learn a certain body of information and then demonstrate that they have learned it. No excuses or playing on the teacher's sympathies will do. In addition, neatness, classroom behavior, and "class participation" are no longer involved in the motivation/evaluation process. Studying is the only way to do well.

4. *TGT is adaptable*. TGT complements, rather than replaces, other kinds of instruction. This means that TGT may be successfully applied in a variety of settings. For example, it is not important how information is first presented—the TGT technique provides practice and over-learning on any material, however it was first learned. This means that TGT can be used in classrooms using individualized instruction, open space, or any other structure, with only minor modification. Because it does not require a new instructional mode, teachers need not be trained in a new way of teaching or in a new philosophy of education. Any teacher can successfully use the technique. TGT is not "teacher-proof," but it can give any teacher a great deal of aid in maintaining motivation and interest in subjects that could otherwise be difficult for children to follow.

TGT does not take the majority of class time. In most of

the experiments reported, TGT activities took no more than 30 percent of the classroom time. More importantly, TGT appears to work both when applied intensively (for example, tournaments every other day) and intermittently (weekly tournaments).

The TGT structure itself can be modified to reflect major differences between students. One simple modification is the provision of especially difficult "bonus" questions for students at the top two or three tournament tables. If ability differences in a classroom are extreme, different games may be played at different tables.

5. *TGT research represents a useful model of research on practical classroom interventions.* Research in methodologies of education often takes one of two approaches. One is highly controlled experiments, either conducted in the laboratory, administered by an experimenter in a classroom, or occasionally administered by a teacher with experimenters directing teacher behavior. The second approach tests instructional methodologies in classroom settings using few (if any) experimental controls. In this model of research, teacher effects, school effects, class effects, and the like are often completely confounded with treatment effects. Further, there is often so little control over the independent variables being manipulated that it is uncertain just what has been done. The well-controlled-experiment strategy is usually high in internal validity, but often has little meaning in terms of application of tested procedures to real classrooms. On the other hand, the poorly controlled classroom research often leaves open multiple, alternative explanations for study findings. In the worst of them (such as those in which teachers volunteer for experimental or control treatments), the conclusions drawn are worthless. However, these experiments can more directly inform classroom practice than can the controlled but laboratory-like experiments, as the treatments used in the

studies are capable of being used in actual classrooms without outside assistance.

The research on TGT has been designed to steer a course between these two models. The evaluative studies of TGT have involved experimental controls, but they have all been interventions administered by teachers in normal classes without extensive outside help. That is, the teacher manuals used in the research can be (and have been) used by teachers entirely by themselves. The experimental controls used have included random assignment of students to treatments at the individual student level in six of the ten TGT studies, and at the teacher or class level in the other four. Teacher and teacher-by-treatment effects have been controlled in several studies by rotating teachers across classes or by statistical means. This research strategy insures a high degree of internal validity, as compared to most classroom studies of instructional methodologies, without reductions in external validity. While the experimental controls are not always perfect, they are at least unbiased. Thus, the consistency of findings across independent studies using procedures which may be flawed in minor but different ways in each study may be interpreted as ruling out alternative explanations of the findings.

The research strategy used to evaluate TGT is one that could be used much more frequently in classroom research on instructional methodologies. It is an inexpensive, practical means of adding to our knowledge of instructional method.

In conclusion, TGT may be seen as representing an unusual event in the history of educational research. It is a technique which arose out of social psychological theory; was exhaustively evaluated in field settings using designs that were high in internal and external validity; and may find its way into educational practice on a mass scale. The evidence collected in the course of research on TGT (see Figure 12) suggests that if this mass acceptance does occur, education at many

Figure 12

Summary of TGT Effects on Students

Study	Subject Area	Student Outcomes			Classroom Process	
		Academic Achievement		Student Attitude	Peer Tutoring	Peer Normative Climate
		Treatment Specific	Standardized Measure			
(1)	Math	+	+	−	−	−
(2)	Math	+	−	+	+	+
(3)	Math	+	−	+	+	0
	Social Studies	0	−	0	0	+
(4)	Math	−	+	+		+
(5)	Social Studies	+ (p < .10)	0	+	+	+
(6)	Language Arts	+	+	0	+	−
(7)	Language Arts	+	+	0	+	−
(8)	Reading-Vocabulary	+	+	−	−	−
(9)	Language Arts	+	0	0	−	0
(10)	Social Studies	0	0	0	+	+

Outcomes 65

levels and in many subject areas may become more effective in increasing the academic achievement, social growth, and mental health of children.

New Developments in Team Learning

The research on the outcomes of TGT is essentially completed, but research on team learning is still continuing at the Center for Social Organization of Schools at Johns Hopkins University and at other sites. This is not the place for a lengthy discussion of this research, but the kinds of issues that have been addressed and are being addressed at present are listed below. For information on any of these topics, please write CSOS at the address listed under Resources (Chapter VI).

- Development and evaluation of team techniques that do not use the tournaments or individual competition.
- Development and evaluation of special-purpose team techniques for the following areas:
    - Social Studies
    - Oral Reading
    - Mainstreaming
    - Class Management
    - Composition Writing
- Further investigation of the effects of team learning on inter-group relations in integrated schools.
- Evaluation of team learning strategies in mixed Hispanic-Anglo schools.
- Evaluation of team learning strategies that make up the bulk of students' instructional day.
- Further investigation of the effects of team learning on student self-esteem.
- Further component analysis to discover which parts of team learning techniques account for their effects, including such components as peer tutoring, equal

opportunities for success, focused schedule of teaching, practice, assessment, amount of team reward, etc.
- Evaluation of combinations of team learning with Mastery Learning.

V.

DEVELOPMENTAL GUIDE

TGT is an instructional design, not a set of curriculum materials. Objectives-based worksheets and games, however, are available from Argus Communications in Niles, Illinois and from the Center for Social Organization of Schools, The Johns Hopkins University, in Baltimore, Maryland.

The materials available from Argus include language arts (grades 4-9), vocabulary (grades 4-6), and verbal analogies (grades 4-6). These materials use card decks with items printed on the cards.

The materials available from the Johns Hopkins Center include language arts (grades 4-9), mathematics (grades 3-8), and nutrition (grades 4-6 and 10-12). These materials use the gamesheet format with decks of number cards.

The development of TGT games for special purposes can be accomplished by referring to several sources which provide banks of objectives and items. They are:

- National Assessment of Educational Progress (NAEP)
  The Education Commission of the States
  1860 Lincoln Street, Suite 300
  Denver, Colorado 80203

- Instructional Objectives Exchange (IOX)
  Post Office Box 24095
  Los Angeles, California 90024

- School Curriculum Objective-Referenced Evaluation (SCORE)
  Educational Services
  Westinghouse Learning Corporation
  Post Office Box 30
  Iowa City, Iowa 52240

- Institute for Educational Research
  1400 West Maple Avenue
  Downers Grove, Illinois 60515

Once appropriate learning objectives have been selected, TGT games can be designed by reference to the following guides (Figures 13, 14, and 15). After developing the games or purchasing them commercially, follow the recommendations in the Design Format chapter, using the GIGS rules.

Developmental Guide 69

Figure 13

What Are Course Objectives?

- Course objectives describe desired outcomes—what the learner should be able to do at the end of a course.

What Are USEFUL Course Objectives?

- A useful objective states what a learner must be able to *do* or *perform* when showing mastery of the objective.

  Useful objectives: Write summary of factors leading to 1929 Depression.
  Be able to solve quadratic equations.
  Repair a carburetor.

  Less useful objectives: Show an appreciation for painting.
  Understand rules of logic.
  Know the rules of football.

- Useful objectives are ones for which separate statements are written for each objective; the more statements, the clearer your intent is made.

Figure 14

Characteristics of Effective TGT Games

(1) ACTIVE LEARNING. When playing the game, all students are constantly involved in answering all questions.

(2) FAST PACED. Students quickly move from item to item, never staying stumped by any given item for long periods of time.

(3) WIN THROUGH SUPERIOR KNOWLEDGE. Students win because they have mastered more thoroughly the specific learning objective taught at the time.

(4) LEARNING WHILE PLAYING. If a student misses an item, there is an opportunity, by reviewing the current answer, to assess the mistake. Knowing that they will face the item again makes learning important.

(5) AGREEMENT ON CORRECT ANSWER. Because the answers are clearly correct or incorrect, students focus on the principles being learned.

(6) PERFORMING IN THE PRESENCE OF PEERS. Students share their successes with two classmates, a highly motivating process.

(7) TANGIBLE SUCCESS. By collecting cards and counting points, students have obvious evidence of their success. Performance on abstract concepts is quickly translated into tangible evidence.

Figure 15

Aids for Successfully Designing TGT Games

At the game level...

(1) Design each game around one objective.

Review games can address multiple objectives, but at no time should more than four objectives be tackled.

(2) On each game, vary the difficulty of items.

Bloom's taxonomy may be useful for analyzing difficulty level. Knowledge (definition, recall), comprehension (convert, explain), and application (draw on facts, principles for solution) are three levels often used in classrooms.

(3) Use no fewer than 20 and no more than 40 items per game.

(4) Always check to see if game (a) requires appropriate level of reading skills, (b) is free of cultural bias, and (c) measures the skills or principles you set out to measure.

At the item level...

(1) Use items for which clearly correct and incorrect answers can be given.

(2) Use items which can be solved within one minute.

(3) Avoid using true-false items (lucky guessers can win too many!).

(4) When using multiple-choice format, create no less than three and no more than four alternative answers.

(5) Keep items brief.

Two short sentences should be the maximum length in stating the problem.

(Continued on Next Page)

Figure 15 (Continued)

(6) Keep the reading level required to understand the items to an absolute minimum (unless reading skills are the focus of the game).

Use a vocabulary which assumes a reading level at least three grade levels below that with which you are working. Use simple, direct language. Use words such as "write" or "say." Avoid "express" or "formulate."

(7) For multiple-choice items, be sure that correct answers fall evenly across all alternatives.

For example, if you have three alternatives, be sure that approximately 33 percent of the items have alternative "A" as correct, 33 percent have "B," and 33 percent, "C."

(8) When using a multiple-choice format, avoid strings of items in which a pattern for correct answers emerges.

For example, if the first six items all have answer "A" as correct, students will easily memorize answers.

(9) Don't lift items from textbooks.

(10) Avoid negatives and double negatives.

(11) Avoid trouble words—*always, often, much*, or *none*.

(12) Whenever possible, the stem of the item should come first, the space for the answer last.

(13) All answers should be plausible.

(14) Answers should be arranged in chronological order or magnitude.

(15) Watch out for the syntax of answers (unless the game involves syntax).

All words should be consistent—if one answer is an adjective, all should be adjectives.

VI.

RESOURCES

Teams-Games-Tournament was developed and validated by David DeVries, Keith Edwards, and their associates at the Center for Social Organization of Schools at Johns Hopkins University in Baltimore, Maryland, under funding from the National Institute of Education. TGT materials are published by Argus Communications and by the Johns Hopkins Center.

Further development and dissemination of TGT are being done by the Center for Social Organization of Schools, The Johns Hopkins University, under continuing funding from the National Institute of Education and the U.S. Office of Education's National Diffusion Network.

PUBLICATIONS

DeVries, D.L., and Edwards, K.J. Learning Games and Student Teams: Their Effects on Classroom Process. *American Educational Research Journal,* 1973, *10,* 307-318.

DeVries, D.L., and Edwards, K.J. Student Teams and Learning Games: Their Effects on Cross-Race and Cross-Sex Interaction. *Journal of Educational Psychology,* 1974, *66,* 741-749.

DeVries, D.L., Edwards, K.J., and Slavin, R.E. *Journal of Educational Psychology,* 1978, *70,* 356-362.

DeVries, D.L., Edwards, K.J., and Wells, E.H. *Teams-

Games-Tournament in the Social Studies Classroom: Effects on Academic Achievement, Student Attitudes, Cognitive Beliefs, and Classroom Climate.* Center for Social Organization of Schools, Johns Hopkins University, 1974(a). Report No. 173.

DeVries, D. L., Edwards, K. J., and Wells, E. H. *Team Competition Effects on Classroom Group Process.* Center for Social Organization of Schools, Johns Hopkins University, 1974(b). Report No. 174.

DeVries, D. L., Lucasse, P. R., and Shackman, S. L. *Small Group Versus Individualized Instruction: A Field Test.* Center for Social Organization of Schools, Johns Hopkins University, forthcoming.

DeVries, D. L., and Mescon, I. T. *Teams-Games-Tournament: An Effective Task and Reward Structure in the Elementary Grades.* Center for Social Organization of Schools, Johns Hopkins University, 1975. Report No. 189.

DeVries, D.L., Mescon, I.T., and Shackman, S.L. *Teams-Games-Tournament in the Elementary Classroom: A Replication.* Center for Social Organization of Schools, Johns Hopkins University, 1975. Report No. 190.

DeVries, D. L., Mescon, I. T., and Shackman, S. L. *Teams-Games-Tournament (TGT) Effects on Reading Skills in the Elementary Grades.* Center for Social Organization of Schools, Johns Hopkins University, 1975. Report No. 200.

DeVries, D.L., and Slavin, R.E. Teams-Games-Tournament (TGT): Review of Ten Classroom Experiments. *Journal of Research and Development in Education,* 1978, *12,* 28-38.

Edwards, K. J., and DeVries, D. L. *The Effects of Teams-Games-Tournament and Two Structural Variations on Classroom Process, Student Attitudes, and Student*

Resources

Achievement. Center for Social Organization of Schools, Johns Hopkins University, 1974. Report No. 172.

Edwards, K. J., DeVries, D. L., and Snyder, J. P. Games and Teams: A Winning Combination. *Simulation and Games*, 1972, *3*, 247-269.

Hulten, B. H. *Games and Teams: An Effective Combination in the Classroom*. Paper presented at the Annual Meeting of the American Educational Research Association, Chicago, April 1974.

Slavin, R. E., DeVries, D. L., and Hulten, B. H. *Individual vs. Team Competition: The Interpersonal Consequences of Academic Performance*. Center for Social Organization of Schools, Johns Hopkins University, 1975. Report No. 188.

IN USE AT

TGT is used nationwide. It is presently used in approximately 30 states and in close to 300 school systems.

WORKSHOPS

One-day TGT workshops are conducted at regional sites. Contact Mr. John Hollifield, The Johns Hopkins University, Center for Social Organization of Schools, 3505 North Charles Street, Baltimore, Maryland 21218.

MATERIALS

TGT games and teaching materials are available from Argus Communications, 7440 Natchez Avenue, Niles, Illinois 60648, and from the Johns Hopkins Team Learning Project, 3505 N. Charles Street, Baltimore, Maryland 21218.

VII.
APPENDIX A

Sample Items from Games Based on GIGS

Appendix A

Sample Items from a Science Game Based on GIGS*

Background of the Game: The students in a seventh grade science class were studying the various life processes. In the game, they were asked to identify each item as one of seven basic life processes.

> A puppy drinks some water.
> (B-9)

> A frog swallows a fly.
> (B-6)

> When you touch a stove, you pull your hand away quickly.
> (B-11)

> A snake lays two eggs.
> (B-24)

Life Processes Game
Answer Sheet

B-1 Hormone control	B-15 Reproduce
B-2 Breathing	B-16 Breathing
B-3 Get rid of wastes	B-17 Digest food
B-4 Reproduce	B-18 Hormone control
B-5 Respond	B-19 Get rid of wastes
B-6 Take in food	B-20 Get rid of wastes
B-7 Take in food	B-21 Digest food
B-8 Digest food	B-22 Breathing
B-9 Take in food	B-23 Hormone control
B-10 Respond	B-24 Reproduce
B-11 Respond	B-25 Digest food
B-12 Reproduce	B-26 Take in food
B-13 Hormone control	B-27 Get rid of wastes
B-14 Respond	B-28 Breathing

*This game was developed by the authors in cooperation with Carolyn Chanoski, a teacher at Northern Parkway Junior High School, Baltimore, Maryland.

Sample Items from an English Game Based on GIGS*

Background of the Game: The students in a seventh grade English class were studying sentences. In the game, they were asked to identify the item as either a complete or an incomplete sentence. If the item was an incomplete sentence, the player had to tell *why* it was incomplete. A sentence was incomplete because either the verb or subject was missing.

We stopped for lunch. (B-4)	A clown and monkey rode at the head of the parade. (B-24)
Leaving the lake in the morning. (B-3)	Leaned out the window. (B-23)

Sentences Game II
Answer Sheet B

B-1 Complete sentence	B-13 Complete sentence
B-2 Complete sentence	B-14 Complete sentence
B-3 Incomplete sentence; no subject	B-15 Incomplete sentence; no subject
B-4 Complete sentence	B-16 Complete sentence
B-5 Incomplete sentence; no verb	B-17 Complete sentence
B-6 Incomplete sentence; no verb	B-18 Incomplete sentence; no verb
B-7 Complete sentence	B-19 Incomplete sentence; no subject
B-8 Complete sentence	B-20 Complete sentence
B-9 Incomplete sentence; no verb	B-21 Incomplete sentence; no verb
B-10 Incomplete sentence; no verb	B-22 Incomplete sentence; no subject
B-11 Incomplete sentence; no verb	B-23 Incomplete sentence; no subject
B-12 Incomplete sentence; no subject	B-24 Complete sentence

*This game was developed by the authors in cooperation with Carol Hopkins, a teacher at Northern Parkway Junior High School, Baltimore, Maryland.

Appendix A

Verb Forms (Game K)
Worksheet

Name _____

Date _____

Class _____

No. Correct _____ Team _____

OBJECTIVE: Change verbs from present to past tense and identify verbs as regular or irregular.

INSTRUCTIONS: This worksheet will help you prepare for the Verb Forms (Game K). Each sentence contains a blank space and a verb to fill in the blank. Write the past tense of the verb, and write whether the verb is regular or irregular. Use the following rules to help you:

Regular verbs form their past tense by adding *ed* to the infinitive.

Example: Talk–talked; work–worked

Some regular verbs have to be slightly changed before forming the past tense.

1. Drop the final *e* before adding *ed*.

    Example: Gripe–griped (not gripeed)

2. When the infinitive ends in *y* preceded by a consonant, change the *y* to *i* before adding *ed*.

    Example: cry–cried (not cryed)

3. When the infinitive ends in one consonant preceded by one vowel, *double the consonant* before adding *d, if* the word has only one syllable *or if* the last syllable is stressed.

    Example: (stop–sto*pp*ed), but, happen–happened
    (First, *not last* syllable is stressed. Don't double the consonant!)

Irregular verbs do not form their past tense by adding *ed* to the infinitive. The only way to learn the past tense of an irregular verb is to memorize it and practice it frequently until it becomes familiar.

My father (*work*) in a bank all his life. K-1	The passengers were excited when the captain (*sight*) land. K-7	After the tennis match, Susan (*drink*) a glass of lemonade. K-13
The lake (*freeze*) last week. K-2	When his mother wasn't looking, Mark (*snatch*) a cookie from the jar. K-8	The children (*run*) down the street trying to follow the fire truck. K-14
The girl (*sing*) the song well. K-3	With a spectacular leap, the outfielder (*catch*) the ball. K-9	The sheriff (*gun*) the criminal down while riding on a horse. K-15
After he (*peel*) the orange, he threw away the rind. K-4	The school (*send*) the students' report cards to their parents. K-10	Barbara's father (*bring*) his lunch with him to work last week. K-16
The thief (*steal*) the money. K-5	Jack's father (*mend*) the holes in his socks. K-11	The stranger (*ring*) the doorbell, but no one answered. K-17
Martha and her sister (*fight*) frequently when they were little. K-6	The teacher (*think*) that the class enjoyed the film. K-12	Bill (*dig*) the garden in April. K-18

Appendix A

The dog (*chase*) after the cat and frightened it. K-19	John found a good recipe and (*bake*) a chocolate cake. K-25	John (*pose*) for the photographer but moved just as the picture was taken. K-31
The teenagers (*enjoy*) themselves on the beach but got sunburned. K-20	The campers used backpacks and (*carry*) their equipment on their backs. K-26	The boys (*hide*) behind the sofa. K-32
My father (*forget*) to bring his keys with him yesterday. K-21	Jane (*reach*) as high as she could but still couldn't remove the book from the shelf. K-27	The mechanic (*loosen*) the screw with a wrench. K-33
The baby (*speak*) in nonsense words. K-22	Mr. Wilson (*teach*) sixth grade for 15 years. K-28	Sandra's grandfather (*die*) five years ago. K-34
The shower (*leak*) all week until the plumber fixed it. K-23	Jane (*choose*) a cola to drink. K-29	Bill (*hear*) the alarm clock ring but still didn't get out of bed. K-35
The children sat in the sandbox and (*make*) castles. K-24	Hansel and Gretel (*lose*) their way in the woods. K-30	Who (*put*) the book on the wrong shelf yesterday? K-36

Mr. Roberts (*sell*) the car but lost money on the deal. K-37		
Jack (*hold*) his baby sister in his arms and fed her. K-38		
Susie had a fever and (*stay*) in bed all day. K-39		
St. George (*slay*) the dragon. K-40		

Appendix A

Answer Sheet

Item	Past Tense	Regular Irregular	Item	Past Tense	Regular Irregular
K-1	worked	regular	K-21	forgot	irregular
K-2	froze	irregular	K-22	spoke	irregular
K-3	sang	irregular	K-23	leaked	regular
K-4	peeled	regular	K-24	made	irregular
K-5	stole	irregular	K-25	baked	regular
K-6	fought	irregular	K-26	carried	regular
K-7	sighted	regular	K-27	reached	regular
K-8	snatched	regular	K-28	taught	irregular
K-9	caught	irregular	K-29	chose	irregular
K-10	sent	irregular	K-30	lost	irregular
K-11	mended	regular	K-31	posed	regular
K-12	thought	irregular	K-32	hid	irregular
K-13	drank	irregular	K-33	loosened	regular
K-14	ran	irregular	K-34	died	regular
K-15	gunned	regular	K-35	heard	irregular
K-16	brought	irregular	K-36	put	irregular
K-17	rang	irregular	K-37	sold	irregular
K-18	dug	irregular	K-38	held	irregular
K-19	chased	regular	K-39	stayed	regular
K-20	enjoyed	regular	K-40	slew	irregular

VIII.

APPENDIX B

Sample TGT Newsletter

Appendix B 89

SAMPLE NEWSLETTER

The Weekly Planet

4th Week, March 28

FLASH! Fantastic Four Sweeps Language Arts Tournament!

The Fantastic Four was the winning team this week with a total of 22 points. John T., Kris, and Alvin put in outstanding performances for the Four, each contributing six points to their team. Their victory brings the Four to second place in the National League standings, only six points behind the leading Giants!

Hot on the heels of the Fantastic Four were the Brain Busters with 21 points. Anita and Tanya helped the team out with victories at their tables, while Peter tied for first at his. The Brain Busters are still in third place in National League competition, but are moving up fast!

Third this week were the American League Geniuses with 18 points. They were helped out by Kevin and Lisa A., both table winners. Other table winners were Lisa P. of the Daredevils and Mike of the Grammar Haters.

This Week's Scores

1st – Fantastic Four		2nd – Brain Busters		3rd – Geniuses	
John T.	6	Anita	6	Mark	4
Mary	4	Peter	5	Kevin	6
Kris	6	Darryl	4	Lisa A.	6
Alvin	6	Tanya	6	John F.	4
	22		21	Dewanda	2
					22/18

Daredevils		Giants		Chipmunks		Grammar Haters	
Lisa P.	6	Robert	4	Caroline	5	Sarah	2
Henry	2	Eric	2	Jerry	2	Willy	2
Cindi	4	Sharon	2	Charlene	3	Mike	6
Fred	4	Sylvia	4	James	2	Theresa	3
	16		12		12	John H.	2
							15/12

Season's Standings Fourth Week

National League		American League	
Team	Season Score	Team	Season Score
Giants	78	Grammar Haters	74
Fantastic Four	72	Geniuses	65
Brain Busters	66	Daredevils	57
Chipmunks	59		

DAVID L. DEVRIES is Director of Research at the Center for Creative Leadership, Greensboro, North Carolina. He received his Ph.D. at the University of Illinois in Social Psychology in 1970. DeVries engaged in TGT research from 1970-1975 while on the staff at the Center for Social Organization of Schools, The Johns Hopkins University. His career has focused on applying social psychological principles to human behavior in various organizational settings ranging from the corporate, to governmental, to educational. He is currently focusing on issues of managerial behavior through such tools as managerial simulation and performance appraisal.

ROBERT E. SLAVIN is a Research Scientist at the Center for Social Organization of Schools, The Johns Hopkins University. He received his B.A. from Reed College in 1972 and his Ph.D. in Social Relations from Johns Hopkins University in 1975. Dr. Slavin is Director of The Johns Hopkins Team Learning project and continues to be active in research, development, and dissemination of team learning strategies. He has written many articles in research and practitioner-directed journals on team learning and on issues of student motivation and classroom organization.

GAIL M. FENNESSEY is Research Manager of the Classroom Organization project at the Center for Social Organization of Schools, The Johns Hopkins University. She received her B.S. in Elementary Education from Boston State College in 1963. She was formerly President of Academic Games Associates, Inc.; Co-Editor of *Simulation and Games*; an Educational Researcher with the Academic Games Program, The Johns Hopkins University; an Associate Educational Specialist at the University of Chicago; and a teacher in the Baltimore and Boston Public Schools. She has published several articles, simulation games, sets of curriculum materials, and research reports, mostly relating to simulation and non-simulation gaming in education.

KEITH J. EDWARDS, B.Ed., M.A., Ph.D., is currently Professor and Director of Research at the Rosemead Graduate School of Professional Psychology, Biola College, in La Mirada, California. He received his B.Ed. from the University of Wisconsin/Whitewater, in Mathematics and his M.A. and Ph.D. in Educational Research and Statistics from New Mexico State University. He was formerly an Associate Research Scientist at Johns Hopkins University, where he developed the TGT technique with David L. DeVries and associates.

MICHAEL M. LOMBARDO is a Research Scientist and Project Manager at the Center for Creative Leadership, Greensboro, North Carolina. For the past several years, he has been a co-investigator in a research project to develop a complex organizational simulation. Prior to that, he directed the development of educational games to be used with the TGT process and headed the media/publications arm of the Center. Lombardo obtained an Ed.D. from the University of North Carolina at Greensboro.